The Gardens
of The Vatican

The Gardens of The Vatican

Linda Kooluris Dobbs
& Kildare Dobbs

F

FRANCES LINCOLN LIMITED
PUBLISHERS

In Memory of my mother Hortense Kooluris
"One of the chosen ones to live and die
in Isadora's beautiful art."

Irma Duncan

Frances Lincoln Ltd
4 Torriano Mews
Torriano Avenue
London NW5 2RZ
www.franceslincoln.com

The Gardens of the Vatican
Copyright © Frances Lincoln 2009
Text copyright © Kildare Dobbs 2009
Photographs copyright © Linda Kooluris Dobbs 2009
First Frances Lincoln edition: 2009

A catalogue record for this book is available from the British Library.

ISBN 978-0-7112-2970-9

Printed and bound in Singapore

9 8 7 6 5 4 3 2 1

HALF TITLE PAGE
Friendly Romans guided Linda to this keyhole vista, in the locked door of the
Garden of the Knights of Malta.

TITLE PAGE
Hilly drive and head gardener's house in distance.

OPPOSITE
Bird Mosaic, La Casina.

Contents

Map of the gardens 6

In the Vatican Gardens: *An artist's vision of a bachelors' refuge 7*

Photographs *20*

Photographer's Comments *158*

Acknowledgments *159*

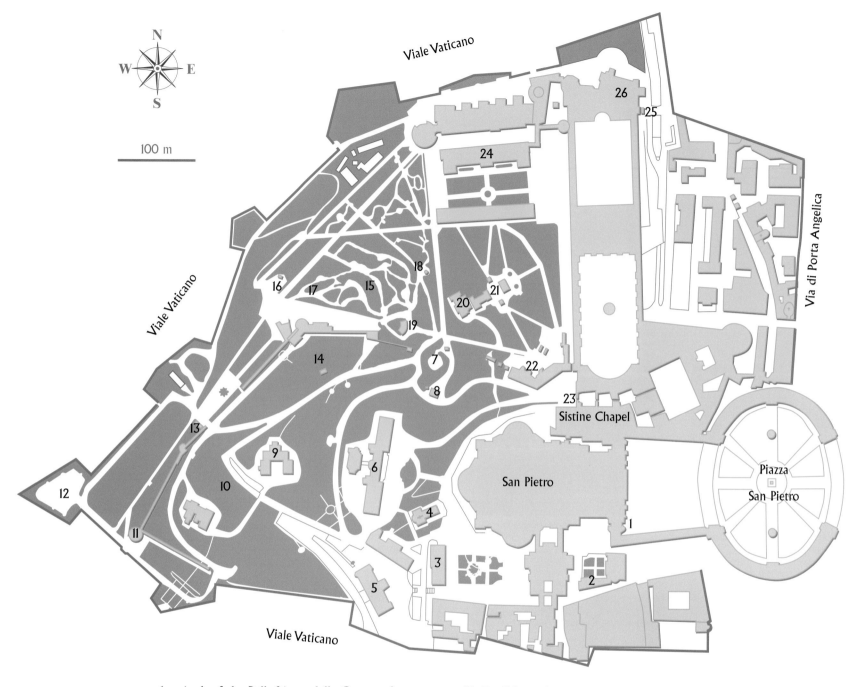

1 Arch of the Bells (Arco delle Campane)
2 Teutonic College
3 Courthouse (Palazzo del Tribunale)
4 Church of Santo Stefano degli Abissini
5 Railway Station
6 Government Palace (Palazzo del Governatorato)
7 Bronze Statue of St Peter
8 House of the Gardener
9 Ethiopian College
10 Italian garden
11 Tower of St John
12 Heliport
13 Grotto of Lourdes
14 Rose garden

15 English garden
16 Chapel of the "Madonna della Guardia"
17 Statue of St Peter in Chains
18 Chinese pavilion
19 Fountain of the Eagle
20 Pontifical Academy of Sciences
21 "Casina" of Pius IV
22 Fountain of the Sacrament
23 Arch of the Sentinel
24 Vatican Pinacoteca
25 Fountain of the Galley
26 Belvedere Palace
   (part of the Vatican Museums)

In the Vatican Gardens

An artist's vision of a bachelors' refuge

Visitors to the Vatican Galleries, when they turn away from the superb works of art on exhibit, may look out of the long windows and catch glimpses of lawns and trees, or intricate parterres with boxwood hedges. Or, climbing to the dome of St Peter's, daunted though they may be by the helical stairs with walls narrowing as they ascend, they may win through to marvellous aerial views. And often they wish they could walk in those pleasant paths shadowed by ancient trees. On bright days the thought may occur that just out of sight – around the corner – there is something wonderful. As it happens, guided tours can be arranged when the gardens are not in use. Visitors will discover their marvels as they stroll through centuries of history.

In the streets around the Vatican the sight of powerful walls and bulwarks seem to suggest that something exquisite is hidden behind them. And from across the Tiber there are inviting glimpses of umbrella pines and other majestic trees within the precincts.

The Vatican gardens in their variety reflect the history of horticulture, even while the visitor is enjoying the guided walk through its green acres. A major pleasure of the tour is provided by the guides themselves, who are not reciting something learned by rote, but speaking out of their personal knowledge and passions.

In the Bible story, the first man was created in a garden, a green shady place between rivers. Water was a precious element to the desert people who wrote the story, and without it there could be no garden. The Bible garden was called Eden or Paradise, the latter word deriving from the Persian for enclosed garden or park. These delightful pleasances even find their way into Persian carpets. Persian miniatures also afford glimpses of flowery retreats. Gardens have been cherished in many cultures as places of rest and pleasure, the most splendid of them also manifesting the importance and wealth of their owners. A glorious example, derived from Persian originals, is the Taj Mahal in India, honouring the memory of a beloved wife, in which sublime architecture interacts with the elements of nature, green grass, trees, fragrant flowers and herbs and, not least with water, reflecting-pools and splashing fountains. The sound of water is as refreshing as the sight, and gardeners often created riffles to make the streams chuckle and gurgle.

Under a burning sun, shade, provided by trees or pavilions, was vital to comfort. George Peele, in the reign of Elizabeth I, praised the cool shadows:

Black shade, fair nurse, shroud me and please me.

The Vatican gardens, enclosed by the high walls of the city-state, provide a pleasant refuge for Popes with the sorrows of the world on their shoulders. Here they may walk and say their breviaries in a green solitude. Here they may sit and meditate to the sounds of birdsong and plashing fountains in airs fragrant with sweet herbs and flowers. And there will be times when nightingales pour their music into the evening air; for where there are trees there will be birds. The psalmist invokes the image of swallows building their nests in temples, "even thy altars, O God of Jacob". There have been gardens on the Vatican hill since the days of imperial Rome. Good soil and abundant water made it possible. The water comes splashing in fountains, rustling and tinkling in channels and cascades, glinting in the warm Roman sunlight. And in recent years, evenings bring showers from buried sprinklers. It is like a pouring out of divine grace. Only one use of water is missing. Although many monasteries practiced pisciculture in fish-ponds, there are no such ponds here. There has never been a need for them, the sea being so close at hand.

This ground was always numinous. Before the empire, the site was sacred to the earth goddess Cybele, worshipped in orgiastic rites by a corps of dancing eunuchs. Her annual festival was first in the Roman calendar. She is still remembered in the gardens, as we shall see.

In Etruscan times, the hill was the resort of prophets or 'vaticinators'. They left only the name Vatican.

It is noticeable that by far the most images and shrines in the Vatican gardens still celebrate the female principle in the person of the Blessed Virgin Mary, whom the Greek Orthodox Church calls Panaghia, Mother of God. It is possible to view this veneration of the female, exalted almost to semi-divinity, as a kind of nostalgia induced by celibacy. At the same time, as we shall see, the actual women of the Vatican, nearly all professed nuns, are valued as hand-maidens, cultivating gardens and providing food.

During the reign of Caesar Augustus the great city was surrounded by the gardens of rich patricians, to which Augustus added a public one. The gardens of Lucullus, who had campaigned in Mesopotamia, were famously Persian, and himself called "Xerxes in a toga". A survivor from the classical era is Hadrian's Garden in Tivoli. Agrippina the Elder, mother of the psychopathic emperor Caligula, made a garden on the Vatican hill that reached all the way down to the Tiber. Another part of the territory was occupied by a circus where Caligula, and later Nero, liked to feed Christians to the lions. All too literally, the blood of the martyrs was the seed of the church. According to tradition, St Peter himself was martyred here, crucified upside down by his own request.

Strolling here, one recalls that from earliest times, holy men took pleasure in nature. Buddhist saints walked with their disciples in a garden; the Muslim paradise is a well-watered garden; St Augustine met with friends in a garden at Hippo, and some sayings of Christ himself reveal love of nature: "Consider the lilies of the field, how they grow. They toil not, neither do they spin; and yet I say unto you that even Solomon in all his glory was not arrayed like one of these."

Not much is known of the Vatican gardens in the Dark Ages between the fall of Rome in the fifth century and the Middle Ages. The empire disintegrated into chaos, with feuding warlords and robber barons. In the ninth century, Pope Leo IV built the Leonine walls to defend St Peter's basilica against invading Saracens. In 846, Muslims had invaded Rome, looted St. Peter's Basilica, and stolen all the gold and silver in it. In response, Pope Leo IV began to build the Leonine walls in 847, completing them in 853. In the late ninth century the Byzantines and Franks together launched an offensive against the Saracens in southern Italy, driving them out. But it was not until the reign of Nicholas III in the thirteenth century that the Popes adopted the Vatican as a permanent residence, albeit one among several. Nicholas had the estate surrounded by new walls and bastions, also making a kitchen-garden, an orchard and a wood. (Nicholas, a strong politician, was consigned by Dante, who accused him of simony, to the eighth circle of hell, which seems rather harsh for a pontiff who grew leeks, onions and cabbages.) There is still a walled kitchen garden to provide fresh produce for the Pope's table. It can be seen from the dome. It is cultivated by Carmelite nuns, each of whom must serve five years at the work. Thus the pontiffs, like many other bachelors, depend for their comforts on the work of self-denying women.

In the tempestuous Dark Ages and later mediaeval times, a garden was most often a small patch surrounded by high walls within the precincts of a castle, essentially a green lawn sewn ("enamelled") with single flowers like a tapestry (see the ground of the famous unicorn tapestries in the Cluny Museum of Paris). Such gardens are limned in the margins of Books of the Hours, with lavish use of gold leaf, illustrating the tasks of horticulture according to the season. Nan Fairbrother, in her classic *Men and Gardens*, comments on the pathos of mediaeval life: "It is such a tiny plot that men have claimed for their pleasure, such a humble unpretentious square they have set aside for happiness, they asked so little . . . " Beyond the ramparts were war, plague, pestilence and famine.

The next Pope, Nicholas IV, added a physic garden, "a garden of simples" or medicinal herbs, the first botanical garden in Italy. We remember that the Church contained all learned professions, including law and medicine. The monk Walafrid Strabo (808–49) describes the herbalist's work. "He digs up the tangled roots of nettles, a weed. He encloses his raised bed with planks to prevent the soil from washing away.

He plants from seed and cuttings and waters them drop by drop – 'with my own hands letting the water run through my fingers' – so as not to disturb the seed by the rush of the water. He grows sage, rue, southernwood, gourd, melon, wormwood, horehound, fennel, iris, lovage, chervil, lily, opium poppy, tansy, catmint, and roses."

To the mediaeval eye, everything was symbolic. There were sermons in flowers. The withering of perennial plants in winter and their rebirth in spring spoke of resurrection. Every herb and tree had its significance: the lily was purity, an attribute of the Virgin, the violet hung its head in humility, the marigold, which maidens used to dye their hair, was, of all things, obedience. Water itself was holy. The very grass whispered its intimations of mortality.

The garden itself could be an emblem of the love Christ bore to the Church. Celibates reading the *Song of Songs* flinched from recognizing a dramatic poem of fervent erotic love. It had to be an allegory for something more spiritual. The closed garden of the poem, with its central fountain, was *hortus conclusus*, an image of virginity.

With the Renaissance, new interest in classical literature and art brought Greek and Latin myth to gardens, where allusion was often to the stories of pagan gods and heroes. Statuary served to strengthen memory, along with fountains, artificial cataracts and a nymphaeum, or water-theatre honouring spirits that haunted springs, lakes and rivers. But the most essential feature was still a lawn of green grass, wrote Albertus Magnus in about 1260, "for the sight is no way so pleasantly refreshed as by fine and close grass kept short". Boccaccio in his *Decameron* also observes that the most praised aspect of a garden in the fourteenth century was "a lawn of very fine grass". And as recently as the nineteenth century, the American poet Walt Whitman sang of grass:

I guess it must be the flag of my disposition, out of hopeful green stuff woven.

Or I guess it is the handkerchief of the Lord,
A scented gift and remembrancer designedly dropt,
Bearing the owner's name someway in the corner, that we may see and
*   remark, and say* Whose?

Even today, the most striking feature of the Vatican gardens is a wide spread of well-mown lawn, the basic green of this peaceful retreat. It is shaded by other greens, the assorted verdure of splendid trees, mostly evergreens, brought from all over the apostolic world, emblems of the universal church. Green is also the colour of hope – along with faith and loving-kindness one of the essentials of Christian aspiration.

Green is the most noticeable feature to visitors in all seasons. The Mediterranean climate tends to be equable and mild, except in the heat of mid-summer, with small changes through the year. In spring and summer, great splashes of colour break out in the gardens as herbs, shrubs and trees come into flower. The calendar of the Christian year is expressed in the changing liturgical colours of clerical vestments in the great basilica of St Peter, with perennial verdure in the gardens.

In the open air, it is the light that changes, crystal clear in winter, in spring soft and misty, while in autumn the fabric of ancient buildings glows with a golden radiance.

What Michel de Montaigne noticed above all in gardens of the Italian Renaissance were fountains, water organs and other curiosities. The Vatican is well supplied with fountains though the frivolity of water surprises is absent. Splashing water cools the air in the sultry heat of Roman summer. And when it rains, it rains, a torrential downpour reminiscent of the tropics.

Many gardens, like those of ancient Rome, were enclosed in a peristyle, an arcaded cloister where the religious would study and wash themselves at ornate basins. Sweet herbs and flowers were grown in these courts, while some of them were laid out in geometrical patterns of low box hedges, often centering on a fountain.

There were gardens in these years between the Middle Ages and the Enlightenment of the eighteenth century which told a story, an allegory of the soul's progress, leading the visitor along paths that ran between hedges of box or myrtle or sweet-scented rosemary and lavender, marked by symbolic statuary and topiary. Some also featured labyrinths or mazes. Such a garden is imagined in Geoffrey Chaucer's *Roman de la Rose*, an allegorical garden of delight, ruled by the god of love. (This garden has been interpreted as an image of the royal court or, in other words, of civilization.) It is a quest of initiation leading to a beloved rose, a vision of perfect beauty. Poets imagined other ideal gardens of the kind. The memory of such an initiatory garden is still found at Bomarzo, castle of the powerful Orsini family, on the road from Milan to Orta, a beautiful village by the lake of the same name, which means "garden".

At the bell-tower entrance to the Vatican, one encounters Swiss Guards bearing halberds and clad in vivid stripes of blue and yellow; and one seems to have stepped far back in time. The uniforms are said to have been designed by none other than Michelangelo, but earlier images show that the uniforms were in existence before his time. Against the south wall of St Peter's basilica is the square of the Roman proto-martyrs, site of Nero's circus where the entertainment was watching Christians being slaughtered. No garden here, with its sorrowful memories, but behind two-storey walls to the west is the flowery cemetery of the Teutons, a quadrant garden crossed by gravel walks, shaded by palm, laurel and cedar and tended by German sisters of Christian Charity. It was given in the eighth century by the Holy Roman Emperor Charlemagne to honour German pilgrims fatigued to death by the long journey from beyond the Alps. They were drawn, perhaps, as much by the soft Mediterranean airs as by the Holy See. Dwellers in the chills of the north longed for the warm south. Centuries later Goethe would sing, *Know'st thou the land where the citrus blooms?* — And before him Andrew Marvell had rhymed in England:

He hangs in shades the Orange bright,
Like golden Lamps in a green Night.

The long journey on foot or on mules over the Alps was arduous and often dangerous. Highway robbery was a favourite occupation of wild men far from towns. But these pilgrims, after their labours, had found only eternal rest in this cemetery. A small church adjoins. The cemetery is one of the oldest of the Vatican's several gardens, each reflecting the age in which it was imagined.

Critics have complained that this plurality of gardens and styles is a defect, that the result is whimsical and leads to loss of unity. But surely the surrounding trimmed lawns and fine trees draw all into harmony. And there is nothing wrong with variety. The absence of sharp boundaries gives one a sense of the indivisible flow of time and history.

Horticulture of a special kind is seen in front of the Governor's Palace, where the reigning Pope's armorial bearings are depicted by intricate planting of variously coloured leaves and flowers. One is reminded of Andrew Marvell's *The Garden,* in which he describes a floral clock. This is a skill associated with Italian gardens, continued in the patterns of low box hedges around the Shell Fountain and in an elaborate geometric parterre nearby, with similar hedges, and in a full-blown labyrinth or maze reminiscent of the initiatory gardens of the Renaissance.

It is convenient here to explain that the Governor's Palace is the administrative centre of the Vatican city-state, 44 hectares of territory in Rome enclosed by high walls. Independence from Italy was declared in the Lateran Treaty of 1929. The Governor, a cardinal, oversees the Gendarme Corps, Utilities, Health and Welfare, Goods and Supplies, Pontifical Villas, Communications and the Philatelic and Numismatic Office. The Pope is absolute sovereign, combining the functions of executive, judiciary and legislature. It may be remarked that it is an unusual kind of state that has no native citizens, no marriages and where every subject is an immigrant. It is a city of bachelors and spinsters, a community of transient celibates, the sole electorate being the cardinals who choose the Pope. The city issues its own stamps, runs its own radio and railway station and sends its diplomats (called Nuncios) to many countries. There are a Vatican bank, and two security forces, the glamorous Swiss Guards and the armed Gendarmes in sober blue. All such services are run by the cardinal-governor, including the grounds, with their 37 gardeners under a director.

The several gardens in the Vatican territory reflect the history of gardens in general. In addition to the quadrant gardens of the Teuton Cemetery and the Square or Secret garden, adorned with lemon-trees in pots, which show Persian influence, there are gardens in the Italian, French and English styles. There is also a rose garden. Sir Francis Bacon wrote in Tudor times of such retreats: "And because the breath of flowers is far sweeter in the air (where it comes and goes like the warbling of music) than in the hand, therefore nothing is more fit for that delight, than to know what be the flowers and plants that do best perfume the air. Roses, damask and red, are fast flowers of their smells; so that you may walk by a whole row of them, and find nothing of their sweetness; yea though it be in a morning's dew". He never smelled these roses! For even sweeter fragrance one has to go to the French garden with its arches of jasmines.

In a far-off corner of the domain, removed from the customary walks and paths, an area is maintained to grow flowers to cut for decorating Vatican interiors. Here too are the seed-beds and forcing frames used in propagation.

A Chinese pavilion, given by the Catholics of that country, represents the Orient. It emanates a peaceful aura, a place to pause and rest. (For an image of a real Chinese garden, one would need to look at a willow-pattern plate and understand *feng shui*.)

An avenue of olive-trees leads from the Grotto di Lourdes to the Vatican Radio, ancient trunks gnarled and twisted yet still bearing. One of them, especially venerable, is a transplant from Gethsemane in the Holy Land, a beautiful place with the ruins of a fine classical synagogue. The olive, symbol of peace, reminds one of the ancient Mediterranean culture, based on the cultivation of vines, olives and wheat. The psalmist said it, "Wine that maketh glad the heart of man, oil to give him a cheerful countenance and bread to strengthen man's heart."

The character of these gardens is informed by the view its creators took of nature. In the Middle Ages nature was hostile to humans, especially in winter, although as we read in *Piers Ploughman,* "in a somer seson whan softe was the sonne" much pleasure was found in burgeoning flowers and in the song of small birds. Against such fugitive delights were the gloomy doctrines of hellfire, purgatory and of the corruption of mortal flesh — things easy to believe under foul conditions of sanitation and personal hygiene. So smelly were the pilgrims who crowded into the great cathedral at Compostela that the clergy installed a huge thurible swinging from a tall arch at the crossing to sweeten the air with clouds of incense. As for the clergy, it is recorded as proof of his sanctity that the martyred archbishop Thomas à Becket, dining with a great lady in France, shook lice from his sleeve, which luckily turned into pearls on the table. The Roman bath had largely fallen into disuse, though adopted as the Oriental *hammam*. Christians began to think that a hot bath was enervating, and even to believe that Spanish victories over the Moors were achieved by Christian knights because they were unwashed and the Muslim enemy was effete, bathed and perfumed.

The carnage wrought by nature in the Black Death (1347-51) and endemic bubonic plague that flared up at intervals made survivors all too familiar with death, especially distressing since so many believed that these horrors were visited on them for their sins.

At the Renaissance, nature was rehabilitated with the emergence of humanism. Man was the measure of all things. It was in this intellectual climate of 1558 that Pope Pius IV, a Medici from Milan, commissioned

Pirro Ligorio to "build a fountain in the woods" of the Vatican gardens. In fact the Casina of Pio IV is an exquisite small palace richly decorated with mosaic inlays, stucco sculpture and fountains. Reflecting the revival of classical learning, its iconography is all pagan. Here the mythology of ancient Greece is exuberantly celebrated in sculpture, including an image of the wild goddess Cybele, here demurely presiding over a fountain. Pausing before her statue, one is struck by the absence of her classical attributes, twin lions at her feet or drawing her chariot, her sceptre and her tambourine. She has been disarmed and rendered harmless, even benign in this Christian setting.

This palace, much larger than it seems, has always been considered the jewel of the Gardens. The details of its ornamentation are delicately beautiful, rendered in stone, in stucco and mosaic inlays. Recently they have been meticulously restored.

The humanist Pope liked to sit in the Casina and talk about poetry and philosophy with his architect. Unfortunately his reign lasted only four years, so that the work had to be completed by his successor. Even before its recent restoration, this was a place of singular beauty.

The Casina centres on a nymphaeum or water theatre in a circular court, with putti and dolphins. There are numerous other fountains in the gardens, requiring lavish amounts of water. In addition, an elaborate sprinkler system keeps the grass and trees green and the air fresh. The history of Roman water supply is a topic too complicated and technical to be introduced here; it is enough to say that among the sources are springs in the Vatican hill, inflows from ancient aqueducts and from the Tiber. A figure of great importance in enhancing the water supply by restoring the Trajan aqueduct was Paul V, a member of the great Borghese family.

Camillo Borghese was a stern, pious and effective pontiff who reigned from 1605 to 1621. He completed the building of St Peter's and made improvements in the Vatican Library. He was accused, like many other popes, of nepotism, placing members of his family in powerful positions. The Borgheses, however, were public-spirited, who used their great wealth for the benefit of Rome. It should be said that nepotism was one of the ways in which a pope could protect his power. In fact, the first pontiff who failed to make his nephews princes was John XXIII. He said, "They dine with the pope once a year. That should be enough for them."

The extra water provided by Paul was badly needed. His Eagle fountain alone, a construction of artificial rock, surmounted by a sculpted eagle and featuring griffins and other fantasies in the grotesque taste of the early seventeenth century, spurts from some thirty jets. Such artificial grottos, perhaps, recall the ancient belief in cthonian powers, gods of the underworld. Then there are the fountains of the Reef – with its rock-garden, of the Shell in the Italian garden, of the Frog in the French garden, of the Sacrament, and elsewhere here and there throughout the domain, not forgetting the most curious of all, a sculpted model of a full-rigged galleon with water spouting from guns and masts. It is magical when floodlit at night. Even without the sprinklers, fountains keep the air fresh.

It may seem a prodigious amount of water for the recreation of one man, and the garden itself an excessively wide domain. "It does seem a bit much," John XXIII once remarked, "but it helps me to remember who I am." John liked to ramble along the pathways and chat with the gardeners or anyone else who happened to be there. His predecessor, Pius XII, wanted solitude, so the gardeners were obliged to hide. But one day during the second world war, after Rome was declared an open city and the German occupiers had withdrawn, Pope Pius encountered a visitor. A young British infantry officer convalescing from a grievous injury received in Sicily was taking light exercise in the gardens. As it happened, he was an Irish Protestant but, being also a gentleman, he bent to kiss the Pontiff's ring. The Pope smiled and asked what he could do for him. The soldier confessed that he himself was not Catholic but that many of his comrades in the Royal Irish Fusiliers were. He took everything out of his pockets and asked His Holiness to bless the whole lot. He would give them all to Catholic friends. The Pope added a personal blessing.

At the present day, the gardens are vacated for security reasons whenever the Pontiff appears, regrettable but no idle precaution in this age of assassins.

For similar reasons public access is limited to guided tours. Pilgrims arrive from the museums watched by gendarmes impeccable in blue; or formerly by bus to the railway station, an obsolescent link with Italy now used to deliver goods. The brief stop here was not so much justified by the handsome building as by the fact that it contains a coin and stamp museum and a duty-free shop. Pilgrims re-entered the bus and were driven to the top of the Vatican Hill, a plateau occupied by the French garden. From here the tour was on foot, by gravel or paved walks.

Visitors may feel that they have stepped out of time, that they are in another, earlier world where all is still and quiet. But if they look up they see the mast of the radio station, or even a modern name like Marconi, and they are aware of the present century with its anxieties.

At first, French gardens were much influenced by Italian models, hence the love of parterres. These patterned beds of earth or gravel, bordered with low boxwood hedges, and shaped by Cartesian geometry, were taken up by the landscape architect André Le Nôtre at Vaux le Vicomte and at Versailles, resulting in vast, humiliating vistas that express dominance over nature and royal or aristocratic power. "Humiliating" may be too extreme an epithet; true, there can be vistas as dispiriting as prairie roads running straight to the horizon, but there are also groves, intimate leafy recesses and bowers. The authors of *The Poetics of Gardening* declare that there are two, and only two, ur-gardens: the enclosed Persian quadrant and the wide-open vistas invented by Le Nôtre. Gardeners of seventeenth-century France preferred flat plains to the sloping sites favoured in Italy and it is characteristic that their four acres in the Vatican are on level ground. But this garden is far from austere, it glows with many flowers, beds of blossoms and oleanders, with fragrant jasmine on trellised arches. We recall that at least one famous French garden, that of the impressionist painter Monet, is richly planted with flowers and water lilies. The artist created his garden to provide subjects for his paintings, organizing nature to celebrate it.

This love of flowers is implicit from Tudor times in English gardens, including a love of wildflowers in their natural setting. Pilgrims pass into the English garden, where nature seems to reign. Shakespeare in his *Midsummer Night's Dream* evokes untamed nature:

I know a bank whereon the wild thyme grows.
Where oxlips and the nodding violet blows,
Quite over-canopied with luscious woodbine,
With sweet musk-roses and with eglantine.

At that time English gentlemen's gardens were formal, adorned with "knots", patterns composed of boxwood and floral elements, in enclosed space. Boundaries vanish in the gardens of Le Nôtre. A spacious royal example of French influence exists at Hampton Court, built for Cardinal Wolsey, given to Henry VIII and enlarged for William and Mary by Sir Christopher Wren. Later it became, as William IV remarked, "a quality poorhouse", housing the widows of great public servants and officers. By the eighteenth century the English park, views from the house often uninterrupted thanks to the sunken fences called *hahas*, were re-arrangements of natural landscapes so that they still looked natural. Avenues of fine trees dramatized the approach to the mansion. The famous landscape architect Capability Brown was in high demand for such parks and gardens, though there were dissenters. One critic told Brown that he wished to die before him: he wanted to see heaven before Brown improved it. The English garden in the Vatican is a continental version of its originals. There just is no room for a great park of the kind found at Richmond or Blenheim.

Yet the air of an English park prevails, with copses of oak by the walls.

By the end of Victoria's reign, British gardens, inspired by romanticism, had become free-form, symphonies of massed flowers and exotic grasses and shrubs. Exceptions were the formal gardens of landscape architects like Gertrude Jekyll, working with Sir Edwin Lutyens, which featured brick walls as well as trimmed hedges. A common feature was the herbaceous border, bright with flowers from all over the temperate world. Lush gardens are found in Ireland and Scotland, in lands warmed by the Gulf Stream, where the growing season is nine months long.

English gardens often feature a temple, a gazebo, a summerhouse, usually of classical type. In the Vatican this element is supplied by the majestic dome of St Peter's, visible all over the domain. It is said that Michelangelo intended the dome to be seen from the Gardens. It may also be seen at a great distance, through a keyhole some kilometres away. With the eager help of passing Romans, the photographer found this view and recorded it. Many of the fountains and other features throughout the territory commemorate historic apparitions and holy places such as

Lourdes, Fatima and Guadaloupe in Mexico. A fragment of the infamous Berlin wall is a reminder of the political skills of John Paul II whose influence helped to loosen the iron grip of Soviet communism and liberate his native Poland. Many exotic trees and plants are gifts from the faithful around the world.

Adjoining the English garden are four acres of fine trees, which some guidebooks grandly call a forest. It is more properly termed a wood, the dark wood of Dante perhaps, where the direct way is lost. In earlier times there were deer and other wild creatures in the gardens where now there are only birds, fewer perhaps than one would find in a more rural setting, not enough of them to excite the curiosity of a priestly ornithologist, but free and welcome. Numbers have been reduced recently by a pair of falcons.

In addition to ornamental structures and architectural features, the Vatican gardens exhibit a number of buildings, ancient and modern. Especially attractive is the Gardener's House, its plain geometry contrasting with the many ornate structures. There is the large Governor's Palace with its offices and chapel, and by the Protomartyrs' Square is the papal auditorium where the Pope holds audiences for pilgrims. Another modern building is the railway station. The ancient Teutonic College adjoins its walled garden and not far away is the oldest church in the Vatican, St Stephen's of the Abyssinians, dating from the eighth century. Here the light falls warmly on textured walls. Beneath it are the ruins of a temple of Vesta. The liturgy is celebrated here by Ethiopian monks, according to the Alexandrine rite of the Coptic church. Two maidenhair or gingko trees from the Orient stand before it. Farther off, there is a convent for the Poor Clare nuns who work in the Vatican.

Other important features include the Tower of St John, the building where John XXIII preferred to work. It is now used as hostel for important guests. Perhaps, like his short-lived successor John Paul I, he was troubled at first by finding himself in an apartment where one flushed the toilet with a gold and diamond handle.

The great scale and extent of these gardens remind us that the Pope was once a great prince in the temporal world whose armies fought battles to defend his realm. At the unification of Italy, the Pope lost his temporal dominions. After Rome fell to the Italian forces in 1871, led by Cavour (its brain), Garibaldi (its sword and muscle), and Mazzini (its spirit), Pius IX remained in the Vatican, claiming that he was a prisoner. Resisting the liberators and forces of Enlightenment, he referred to the insurgents as "brigands". Remaining in the Vatican, the Pope had the gardens re-organized into their present form, preserving the historic origins.

The dispute was settled in 1929 by the Lateran Treaties, sponsored by Mussolini, creating the sovereign city-state of the Vatican. The smallest state in the world, it is also the last absolute despotism in Europe.

A lucky visitor encounters a gardener, his eye contemplating a tree. He is pondering whether it needs pruning. His clear, tanned features recall a Raphael model.

A final stop is once more at the delightful Casina, already noticed, which carries imagination back to pre-Christian times, with its gods and goddesses in marble and stucco, essentially personifying the forces of nature. The interaction of Greek philosophy with Christian revelation, of reason (*logos*) with faith, happens to be a topic that interests Pope Benedict XVI. He is less interested in the myths. The Casina is now the seat of the Pontifical Academy of Sciences, which includes many Nobel prize-winners around the world, and other eminent scientists, not all of them Roman Catholics. At one meeting, some years ago, John Paul II ruled that the savants could discuss anything *after* the big bang. They were not to look further back for the creation. Whereupon Stephen Hawking went home and did some fancy sums that led him to postulate a universe without beginning or end.

The magnificence of the Pope's palace and art collections had declared and exhibited his power. In the same way his flourishing and beautiful estate with its fountains and gardens had been symbols of might and authority.

The authority now claimed for him is spiritual, not of this world, and perhaps no better emblems of that claim could be found than in works of art and nature. The shepherd of souls is, like Adam, also a gardener maintaining things green and growing in his care. The diligence with which they are nurtured and cultivated figures forth the cure of human souls, the outward signs of a devoted pastor.

Above all, in their beauty and health, the gardens are to declare and praise the glory of God. In the Psalmist's words from the dawn of poetry:

Praise the Lord upon the earth, ye dragons and all deeps;
fire and hail, snow and vapours, wind and storm, fulfilling his
word; mountains and all hills; fruitful trees and all cedars;
beasts and all cattle; worms and feathered fowls; kings of the
earth, and all people; princes, and all judges of the world;
young men and maidens, old men and children, praise the
Name of the Lord. For his Name only is excellent, and his
praise above heaven and earth. He shall exalt the horn of his
people; all his saints shall praise him, even the children of Israel, even the
people that serveth him.*

*Version of Miles Coverdale (1488-1569)

Across the Tiber, a glimpse of Vatican trees beyond the Ponte Vittorio Emanuel II and St Peter's.

Castel Sant'Angelo was originally the tomb of the Roman Emperor Hadrian, dating from A.D.135 to 139. In the 14th century it became a fortress and prison for the Popes. Today it is a museum.

Hadrian also built the Pons Aelius to commemorate his adopted son. It now exhibits a series of baroque angels bearing the emblems of Christ's passion, including this one with a scourging rod.

LEFT Looking east from an apartment building on via Nicolo V at St.Peter's and Roman pines.

RIGHT The Perugina Gate is one of four entrances to the Vatican state, not counting railway access.

Mighty walls surround the Vatican, recalling an embattled past. Yet inside the territory one is seldom aware of the fortifications.

Inevitably these walls, seen from via Nicolo V, arouse
curiosity. What treasures can they be hiding? Deep within
is the cloister of ciphers and secrets, the silence of power.

Looking north over the walls at evergreens and Roman Pines.

LEFT Via della Stazione Vaticana.

OPPOSITE The glorious dome of the basilica rises above walls and pines.

LEFT The Vatican railway is employed for deliveries of food and other necessities. Clearly it is not much used, the tunnel closed, the tracks overgrown.

OPPOSITE The Santo Ufficio Gate, now called the Petrine Gate, is monitored by a Swiss Guard. The design of his blue and yellow uniform dates from the Renaissance. Security duties are shared with a corps of gendarmes, and the Guard no longer has to make war on the Pope's enemies. The Holy Office, with its Inquisition, was formerly feared by dissenters and heretics. To soften this image, its name has been changed to the Congregation for the Doctrine of the Faith. The Roman church is still strong on uniformity, like the Roman Empire before it. Ancient Rome drove its roads dead straight, ignoring the terrain; and standardized the weapons of its legions.

LEFT Visitors begin their tour of the green world with this foretaste of the gardeners' art, nature trimmed by topiary. There's a summery fragrance of mown grass.

OPPOSITE A grinning water-god shows his parched tongue. But where is the water?

PAGES 36–37, LEFT TO RIGHT
Antique figures gratify the Italian love of garden sculpture. The Fountain of the Spinster is the first of these relics of the imperial past.
Bust of a Roman worthy, at the start of a walk near the Square Garden.
Early spring is colouring the garden behind this ancient statue, pagan god, general or emperor.

A fragment of the Berlin wall recalls the influence of John Paul II in bringing democracy to his native Poland, thus triggering a general collapse of totalitarian communism. A reminder that Popes are engaged with history.

The Long Walk, close to the Square Garden, reveals
contours. The Vatican is a hill, cult centre in Pagan times
for the mother goddess Cybele.

Sculptures stand starkly amid a riot of spring flowers.

Morning lights the great basilica behind trees and rising
ground above the level Square Garden. The slope is fairly
steep, as visitors will soon discover as they walk.

Essentially Persian in its austere quadrant centred on a
grand fountain, the Square Garden is overlooked by the
Picture Gallery and St Peter's.

Lemon trees in pots
soften the austerity.

OPPOSITE
ABOVE In morning light the Square Garden is seen without lemon trees in its simplicity. The Picture Gallery is on the left, and in the background is the Palace of the Belvedere.
BELOW Façade of the Picture Gallery.

RIGHT
The fountain and the Picture Gallery's central block. The balcony is open only on private occasions.

The tree of life, a modernist
bronze by Yigsolo, confronts the
classical dome of the basilica.

This elegant gate is the southern entrance to the Square Garden.

Michelangelo designed his great dome to be seen from the gardens. Here is a fine view combining nature and art, the foreground all "amorous green" (Andrew Marvell's phrase) marked with the beautiful, rough bark of a pine tree.

The exquisite Casina of Pius IV, a Renaissance palace with classical iconography, as it is since restoration. Pius IV, a Medici and a humanist, seems to have baptized the nymphs and goddesses. Behind the pond and bank of lilies sits the figure of Cybele, formerly goddess of this place.

As it was when in disrepair.

Begun in 1553 by Pirro Ligorio and Sallustio Perruzzi, the Casina was completed by 1562. Today it houses the Pontifical Academy for Sciences, whose members are distinguished academics from many countries. Cybele with lilies.

Polaroid Transfer of Cybele and bank of lilies suggests a different mood.

The goddess is flanked by images of Christian virtues, the wall richly decorated with mosaics in the style of ancient Rome. The humanist Pope, Pius IV, sought to bring pagan imagery to the service of his faith.

LYMPHÆVM HOC
CONDIDIT·ANTIQVISQVE
STATVIS·EXORNAVIT

LEFT Antique image of Pudicizia, personifying modesty, a quality equally admired by ancients and Christians.

OPPOSITE The mosaics illustrate creatures of earth, water and air: fruit, fowl and fishes, favourite subjects of ancient art – and no less prized at the dinner table. The Casina was probably, among other things, a banqueting house. Its open spaces made it suitable for dining out on hot evenings

Monochrome mosaics of fantastic subjects give a kind of pebbly, rustic effect on the left, announcing the papal builder.

And on the right
images of diners
and flowers.

BELOW

LEFT A Casina fountain spills a lavish overflow of water. From earliest times the Vatican hill was well irrigated from streams and springs, augmented today from aquaducts and the Tiber.

RIGHT In the central fountain of the Nymphaeum, honouring the water spirits, one of two putti rides a dolphin.

OPPOSITE Classical frieze in stucco relief, under its pediment, features caryatids and richly ornamental detail. Pius IV with his classical learning enjoyed the antique idiom. He liked to sit and converse with Ligorio, his architect, in the building.

OPPOSITE Hidden between the two front buildings is the Nymphaeum. The Casina consists of several structures and is bigger than it appears.

LEFT A side view of the first building, flanked by steps, reveals its modest scale.

Moulding in stucco was a more forgiving medium than carving stone and Italian artists excelled at it. In the coming centuries their work was in demand all over Europe and from as far away as Ireland.

Restoring this architectural gem was costly and took three years. Neither the Vatican nor the Italian state funded it. The project, like others undertaken by the museums, was paid for by the Patrons of the Vatican Museums, directed by Father Allen Duston O.P.. Here Father Duston sits to enjoy a quiet moment. His personal qualities have won him friends of many faiths and nationalities, who gave gladly at his request.

LEFT A closer view of Father Duston in his Dominican habit, happy to have helped in the restoration.

OPPOSITE Alcove with statuary and mosaics in the upper courtyard.

More fish and fowl in mosaic, surely
representing a pontiff's menu.

Twin Fish Mosaic, La Casina.

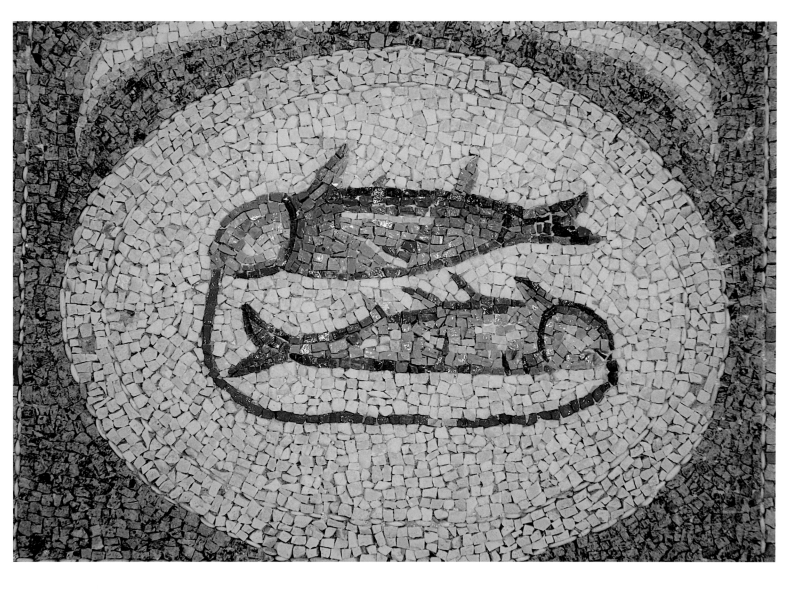

LEFT Entrance to the Casina is through this noble gate.

RIGHT From a window of the Portrait Gallery, visitors see the Casina in its own landscaped garden.

Nose pressed to the pane reveals this larger view.

From the dome of St.Peter's the scale of the Casina is evident. In the background is glimpsed the level Square Garden with its lemon trees in pots.

OPPOSITE The Chinese Pavilion, nestling in lush greenery, is the gift of Catholics of that country.

RIGHT Above the statue of St. Peter in chains shows the saint dejected. This 19th-century work was given to Pope Leo XIII when he declared himself a prisoner of the Vatican.

BELOW A clearer view is seen here.

The Fountain of the Blessed Sacrament honours the holy mass and the reign of a Borghese pope.

PAVLVS·V·PONTIFEX·MAXIMVS
AD·AVGENDVM·PALATII·PROSPECTVS
ET·HORTORVM·DECOREM
FIERI·IVSSIT·PONT·ANNO·IV

It is flanked by twin towers and by a single olive tree.

An avenue of luxuriant palms almost hides the Casina.

The Gardener's House behind tall evergreens and smooth green lawns. Here the head gardener lives, overseeing some 40 gardeners.

LEFT The Gardener's House, with its stark and ancient geometry, exerts a special charm. Far off one may see the radio tower that sends out the Pope's messages to the world.

OPPOSITE A gardener ponders: to prune or not to prune? This young man might have stepped out of a painting by Raphael.

A panel that was originally somewhere else is built into the
wall of the Head Gardener's House. It shows papal insignia
held aloft by putti and flanked by two female figures.

A fragment commemorating the First Vatican
Council depicts alabaster cherubs.

OPPOSITE In the garden amid things green and growing the bronze statue of St. Peter confronts the mighty dome of his basilica. The Spanish poet Federico García Lorca sings "Green how I want you green/ Green wind, green boughs . . ."

ABOVE The image is repeated at right in a Polaroid Transfer, giving the impression of a distant memory.

OPPOSITE A perspective marked in shrubs leads to the Dome.

BELOW A view from the Dome of the garden where Carmelite nuns grow the Pope's vegetables and salads.

OPPOSITE
ABOVE Gift of the
munificent Borghese Pope,
the Fountain of the Eagle is
a fantasy in the grotesque
style of the early 17th
century, spouting clear
water through 30 jets. Seen
with the Convent of the
Poor Clares behind it and
the Marconi tower.
BELOW A closer view.

RIGHT
A mouldering griffin
spouts from his jet.

A modern traffic sign.

The Mater Ecclesiae Convent of the
Poor Clares, Franciscan nuns.

The Vatican radio tower. The Vatican broadcasts in more than 40 languages, its operations managed by the Society of Jesus. Programmes are primarily religious but the arts and public affairs are also included.

Nature disciplined under
the Leonine walls, the
Vatican's earliest ramparts.

ABOVE A dreamer's view of St.Peter's, achieved by Polaroid Transfer

OPPOSITE The Rose Garden in summer and, beyond, the head office of Vatican Radio.

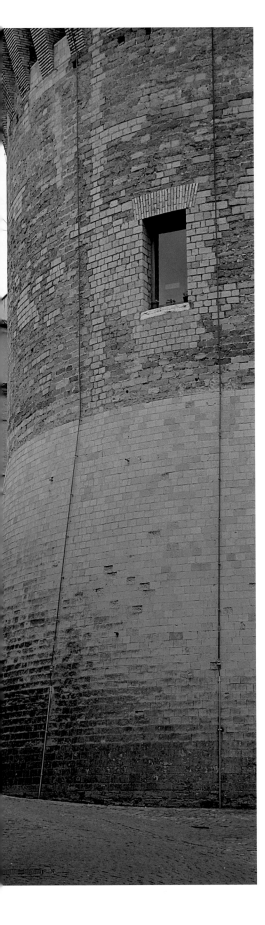

PREVIOUS PAGES, LEFT TO RIGHT
St. John's Tower half hidden by palms. An Irish hymn
invokes God: "Be Thou my high tower," defending
against evil. Pope John XXIII had the building restored as
his preferred residence.
Satellite dish beside the Vatican radio tower, catching
signals from the world.
A level walk to the Leonine Walls and Marconi Tower.

OPPOSITE A saintly bishop (Austremonius) in bronze
stands among greenery in front of St. John's Tower.

LEFT A path by the Leonine Walls.

BELOW The Madonna del Divino Amore (Our Lady of
Divine Love).

Our Lady of
Mercy of Savona.

The Little Temple of
Our Lady of Loreto.

BENEDICTO · XV · P · M · NEOCORI · MARIANI · AB · EXCVBIIS
NOMINE · GENVENSIVM · CIVI · AVGVSTO · DONVM · DEDERVNT

Our Lady of Lourdes in her grotto commemorates an apparition in France, at a site visited by thousands of pilgrims, many sick in hope of a miracle cure.

Portrait of Bishop Schoepfer of Tarbes Lourdes,
instigator of the Vatican grotto.

LEFT

ABOVE Art and nature. Against a backdrop of architecture and topiary, gnarled and twisted branches suggest wild nature.
BELOW The gardener's art exhibits the beauty of flowers

OPPOSITE Topiary archways along the roadside of spring verdure. And could that be a young rabbit on the slope? He could meet with an accident.

PAGES 108–109, LEFT TO RIGHT
Sculpture by Frederick Shradi, the only American work in the gardens, celebrates a famous apparition of the Virgin at Fatima, Portugal. It was given in memory of the attempted assassination of John Paul II, who attributed his recovery to the Virgin. This bell, marking the Jubilee of 2000, was presented by the foundry that cast it. The Marinelli family has been making bells for more than 1,000 years. Sentry box, used in rainy weather.

OPPOSITE Looking over the Vatican wall to a distant observatory

BELOW The heliport from which the Popes normally take off for the Leonardo da Vinci airport.

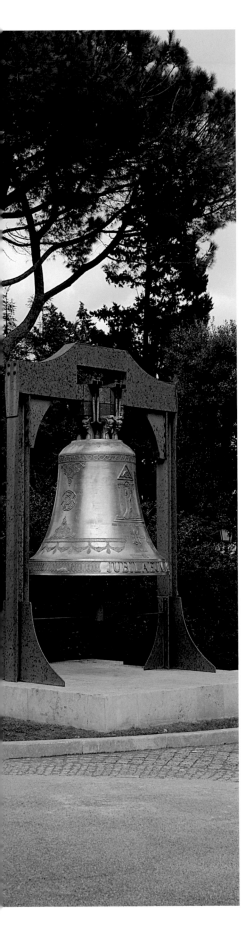

This gnarled and knotted olive-tree was transplanted from
Gethsemane, from the scene of Christ's agony.

An avenue of olives, ancient on the right, reminds
one of the Mediterranean cultivation of wheat,
vines and olives – bread, wine and oil.

LEFT A stone bench, harsh relief for weary old bones.

OPPOSITE Spring brings out a riot of blossoms all through the gardens, quickening the step of aging dignitaries.

ABOVE
A labyrinth in the Italian garden recalls the taste for such curiosities. In the pilgrimage Cathedral of Chartres there is a labyrinth marked on the floor. And the boxwood maze at Hampton Court, near London, has been a famous tourist site since Tudor times.

RIGHT
Another view of the Italian garden, overlooked by the Dome of St. Peter's.

How delightful to walk among these fragrant trees!
Andrew Marvell, the poet of gardens, exclaims:

My Soul into the boughs does glide:
There like a Bird it sits, and sings,
Then whets, and combs its silver Wings . . .

The Ethiopian College in 2005 celebrated
its 75th anniversary.

One of the Pope's titles, of pagan origin, is *Pontifex
Maximus*, i.e. the Greatest Bridge-Builder. The bridge was
a metaphor; actual bridges are few in the Vatican. A
saying of Jesus (Issa), preserved by Muslims, declares,
"Life is a bridge: build no houses but pass over".

This underpass leads to the Railway Station.

Fountain of the Shell is surrounded by patterns of the
low boxwood hedges in the Italian taste.

In the handsome little Railway Station there is a museum
of coins and stamps and a duty-free shop.

The railway, with a rare train, flanked by the Fountain of the Shell with its parterre.

Going nowhere – gates are closed against these coaches.

PAGES 124–125
LEFT The Station has its own fountain, spilling from the lion's mouth.

RIGHT Built-in detail displays the sculpted papal armorial bearings, triple crown and keys of Heaven and Hell.

Such was the happy garden state/ Where man first walked without a mate.(Marvell).

Evening closes in on the bachelors' garden.

Trim box hedges with the heroic South Gates.

Seen from the great dome, the Governor's Palace looks
what it is – a hive of bureaucracy. This is the Vatican's
State's busy administrative centre.

And from ground level, fair and square behind the
parterre with the arms of Pope Benedict XVI.

RIGHT An oblique view of the Governor's Palace is softened by trees, shrubs and parterre with coat of arms of flowers and box hedges in front .

OPPOSITE The pleasing variety of evergreens from around the world with a path of patterned cobbles

OPPOSITE Looking out from the Governor's Palace at the basilica.

ABOVE Rhododendrons blossom and, beyond, a tree puts forth tender leaves. The great dome towers in spring light.

The Arch of the Sentinel.

LEFT Ancient textured walls in the sunburnt umber and ochre of Rome, the via del Governatorato leading from the Pope's apartments.

RIGHT A white-gloved gendarme guards the Arch of the Sentinel. His corps protects security in the Holy See.

LEFT Interplay of grand architecture with cypress tree and plants.

OPPOSITE
ABOVE Rear of basilica with greenery.
BELOW The basilica. Magnificent building with fountain and evergreens: stone, water and vegetation.

Patterned cobbles, topiary, trees and the basilica from the rear.

LEFT St. Stephen of the Abyssinians is
the Vatican's oldest church.

RIGHT Portal of the Tribunal, surmounted by emblems of
papal authority. Note the humble rubbish bin.

St. Catherine of Sienna (1347–1380) was a nun who is credited with a "mystical marriage with Christ". A brilliant theologian, her writings are Italian classics.

St. Marianna of Jesus, also called the Lily of Quito, lived in early 17th-century Peru, spent her life in prayer and was credited with stopping an earthquake and other miracles.

Santa Mariana de Jesús
Paredes y Flores
1618–1645
Ecuador   Pio XII

LEFT Seen from the dome, the Teutonic College and Cemetery founded by Charlemagne (747–814). The luxuriant cemetery is the Vatican's oldest garden. German pilgrims were buried here. The large oval window is part of the Pope's great audience chamber, where he greets and blesses pilgrims.

BELOW Legend claims that St. Peter was crucifed here in the Square of Proto-martyrs. Beyond is an external view of the Teutonic College and Cemetery.

Bernini's great fountain with part of his colonnade
behind it in St. Peter's Square.

These fine young men are the last Swiss mercenaries in Europe. They are chosen for their character and physique, after their military training in the Swiss army.

PAGES 146–147
LEFT In the courtyard of the Belvedere Palace, this global
sculpture by Sicilian sculptor Gio Pomodoro (1930-2002)
is the same size as the ball on top of the great dome of
St. Peter's.
RIGHT The majestic Belvedere Palace is approached by
these steps, with fountain and lions. On top is an
antique bronze pine-cone, once considered the epitome
of beauty, with bronze peacocks, all from the gardens of
Emperor Hadrian.

The Fountain of the Galleon is one of the most pleasing fantasies of the Vatican Gardens. Water spouts from its guns and rigging. Floodlit at night, it seems magical.

LEFT Visitors climbing the last stairs to the dome enjoy this awe-inspiring view of its richly decorated interior.

BELOW Sculptures surmounting Bernini's embracing colonnade include these figures with the Pope's arms, keys and triple crown. This tiara, emblem of worldly dominion, was abandoned by Paul.

BELOW
Perspective of the front of the Apostolic Palace where
the popes live and die.

OPPOSITE
Summer heat is relieved by Bernini's beautiful fountain.

OPPOSITE
At night they are lit by ornate lamps in the Bernini Colonnade.

ABOVE
The Egyptian obelisk, an imperial trophy, fronts this moody view of St. Peter's,
created by Polaroid Transfer.

Evening falls on the Tiber and
the Vatican beyond.

Photographer's Comments

In December 1981, I had my first glimpse of the Vatican Gardens from the walls surrounding and through the Vatican Museums' windows and began my photographic record of that holy setting with a very old and trustworthy Nikon F2 camera.

In May 2000, at the invitation of Father Allen Duston O.P., International Director of the Patrons of the Arts in the Vatican Museums, I went to Rome and spent a week visiting the Gardens and, once the rains stopped, began a serious photographic study of them. *The National Post* newspaper published a travel article of mine, including photographs of that marvellous trip. After learning the technique of Polaroid Transfers and continuing to produce Giclee prints, I did a large exhibition of images produced in those techniques, as well as straight photographic prints at First Canadian Place Gallery and the Joseph D. Carrier, Columbus Centre in Toronto in 2002. It happened to overlap with the Holy Father's visit to the city to celebrate World Youth Day.

In March 2003, while celebrating Father Duston's Silver Jubilee as a priest with my husband, the writer Kildare Dobbs, in dreamlike surroundings, I had the good fortune to have crystal clear light to shoot again and gather more images. Once again *The National Post* published more of my photographs, this time to accompany a travel piece that Kildare wrote. Following that, I realized that I could expand my collection with my newly acquired digital Nikon equipment and I returned in October 2006 to spend another week revisiting the Gardens and seeing the now completely restored La Casina of Pius IV. It was once again a blessed trip that offered up hundreds of successful images.

In March 2008, just before Easter, I returned to Rome and the Vatican to find more views from inside and outside the walls of the Holy See. The weather was very unstable with torrential rains, thunder and hail, and yet, as before, whenever I needed it, the heavens quieted down and I got my shoot. Revisiting the Gardens on the ground offered up new impressions. After taking the elevator, hoping I wouldn't have an attack of claustrophobia, I climbed the 320 remaining steps to the top of Michelangelo's Cupola of St. Peter's. There I found sweeping aerial views of the Gardens and of Rome. I even went so far as to shoot through a keyhole at a distance across the Tiber at the Piazza Cavallieri di Malta where the Knights of Malta have a locked refuge behind high walls. Through a high arch of green leaves in a stunning park one has the perfect symmetrical sighting of the Dome of St. Peter's and green trees that surround it. Twenty-seven years after my first shoot, I felt my collection was complete to create this book.

Linda Kooluris Dobbs, Toronto March 31st, 2008

Acknowledgments

My husband **Kildare Dobbs,** for patience, humour, scholarly research and sensitive writing and the more than a quarter century of love and understanding.

Father Allen Duston O.P., former International Director of the **Patrons of the Arts in the Vatican Museums,** whose belief in me and invitation to photograph the Vatican Gardens and whose grace and hospitality while I was in Rome gave me a muse and set me on a new path in my work.

Thank you to **Romina Cometti** and **Elizabeth Heil** for their insightful knowledge of art history and love of the Gardens.

Gunars Roze, master photographic printer with whom I have worked for over 26 years, who was able to retrieve and enhance my original vision taken on film by producing exquisite results on paper.

Charles Chiu and his staff at **Colourgenics Lab** in Toronto, for years of offering up perfect scans, printing and consistent attention to detail.

Saul Lederman, André Souroujon and **Jason Sansalone at Pikto Lab** in Toronto, who sensitively created a leatherbound presentation book from my digital files of images and design. That enabled others to have a condensed glimpse of the beauty of the Gardens.

Brian George of **Vistek,** for holding my hand as I made the transition from film to digital cameras, allaying my fears as I plunged into that world and for teaching me what I needed to get me started.

Jonathan Williams, my agent, for his belief in this project and hard work getting others to envision it as a book.

To my parents, **Hortense and Spero George Kooluris,** for giving me the example, support and freedom to dream big dreams and develop as an artist.

And to **Becky Clarke, John Nicoll** and his marvellous staff at **Frances Lincoln** for knowing the secrets of alchemy to make this book into gold.